TAKE BACK YOUR LIFE NOW!

MASTER THE TEN TRAITS OF TODAY'S HEALTHY WOMAN

*A Ten-Week Program
That Will Inspire You To BE Your Healthiest!*

By

Dr. Barbara McFarland and Steve Wuest

Illustrated by Ann Telnaes

© 2003 by Dr. Barbara McFarland and Steve Wuest.
All rights reserved.

No part of this book may be reproduced, stored in a retrieval system, or transmitted by any means, electronic, mechanical, photocopying, recording, or otherwise, without written permission from the authors.

ISBN: 1-4107-7916-5 (e-book)
ISBN: 1-4107-7915-7 (Paperback)

Library of Congress Control Number: 2003095847

This book is printed on acid free paper.

Printed in the United States of America
Bloomington, IN

1stBooks – rev. 8/18/03

Contents

Acknowledgements iv

Introduction vi

The Take Back Your Life Program 1

   1. I Am Balanced 9

   2. I Am Confident 21

   3. I Am Fit 33

   4. I Am Humorous 43

   5. I Am Loving 53

   6. I Am Passionate 65

   7. I Am Optimistic 75

   8. I Am Self-Accepting 85

   9. I Am Self-Nurturing 95

  10. I Am Spiritual 107

Final Thoughts 115

Educational Tools 117

About the Authors 120

The Artist 122

Acknowledgements

When we first began working on the ten-trait model, we realized that we had a lot of work ahead of us; however, we had no idea that we would meet the many wonderful and supportive people who were eager and willing to pitch in and give us feedback, participate in focus groups and survey research, and review this manuscript.

So, we'd like to thank Julie Webster, Judy Newport, Tom Hodson, and Susan Cranley for the time they spent reviewing this manuscript; Angela Wilcox, Sandy Kent, Beth Schott, Linda Scott, Rose Mary Tanks, Tokiko Freeman, and Weona Smithmeyer were extremely helpful as they gave us feedback on the characters and the way the traits should be illustrated; Kirsten Stilgenbauer, Carol Trushel, Kathleen Stocker, Paula Stapleton, Myra Avery, Laura Kitzmiller, Suzette Percival Lipker, and Janice Hamilton participated in one of our focus groups for the Today's Healthy Woman poster. And last but not least, Virginia Watson Rouslin whose work in the area of women's health has given us opportunities for networking as well as a significant venue for sharing our message.

A very special thanks to the talented Alta Bradford whose creative juices helped us in more ways than we can say and included introducing us to graphic designer Rita Milbern who was enthusiastic and responsive to our frequent last minute deadlines.

Our book, the Today's Healthy Woman poster, and our other educational and inspirational tools would not be the same without the talent of our gifted Pulitzer Prize editorial cartoonist, Ann Telnaes. Ann's work has been creative and insightful and she has been especially delightful, pleasant, and fun to work with. She exemplifies what team spirit is all about.

Of course, we are most grateful to our families for their understanding and patience while we were often times unavailable and distracted, for their honest feedback when we sometimes didn't want to hear it, and for their unending support of all that we do.

"The nice thing about teamwork is that you always have others on your side."
Margaret Carty

Best of Health to you!

Barbara McFarland, EdD
Steve Wuest

Introduction

Cholesterol levels, blood pressure ratios, blood sugar levels, and bone density scans…although not as sexy as Jennifer Lopez's workout routine for getting tight abs or as fun as the Passionate Vegetarian cookbook, these health screens are becoming a major focus of what I'm reading about in women's magazines and seeing on those glitzy women's health segments on television. Whether it's the most recent study on cardiovascular disease, migraine headaches or hormone replacement therapy, my head is spinning with information about the latest studies, drugs or nutritional supplements that will lead me to better health and I know other women feel the same way. At least that's what I hear from my patients.

As a psychologist who has worked with women for over 20 years, I find it rather interesting that in all of this hoopla on women's health there is very little emphasis on our *mental health* or emotional well-being and the critical role it plays in our overall health. Perhaps the culprit is the cultural taboo regarding mental health and its association with weakness and lack of resilience. Having been categorized as the weaker, more emotional sex for centuries, I suppose that it might not be politically correct to zero in on this part of a woman's health. Focusing on the medical end of things is somewhat less complicated and more easily quantifiable. For example, getting the correct dose and compatible anti-depressant can take months of trial and error attempts whereas blood pressure or cholesterol medication is more easily dispensed.

Yes, I have to admit that I dislike the term "mental health" since it has such negative connotations – fraught with images of weak-willed Prozac junkies who can't seem to get control of their lives. To me, mental health is a phrase that's as outdated as the notion that women are merely homemakers.

So, I prefer to use the phrase *mental wellness* when speaking of women's mental health. It has a more proactive and positive spirit reflecting that our emotional lives are not simply dictated by genetics, PMS, hormones, and faulty cognitive patterns.

As healthcare providers and insurers cite the statistics and preventive measures on cardiovascular disease, osteoporosis, breast cancer, incontinence, and diabetes, all of which have high incidence rates for women, there is very little discussion on the importance of a woman's *mental wellness as a critical factor in overall health.* Depression, for example, affects twice as many women as men. Whether it's genetic, hormonal, relational or cognitive, when a woman is depressed or besieged with anxiety how likely is she to care about her diet, exercise or cholesterol levels?

I think those of us who really care about women's health need to include not only the physical aspects but also what it takes to help women achieve and maintain *mental wellness*. I may be biased but I strongly believe that emotional health is the foundation upon which women's physical well being rests.

I decided to remedy this situation by interviewing women and conducting research that would identify the key traits a woman needs to have in order to be the healthiest she can be. Instead of focusing on the dark side of mental health such as depression or anxiety, etc., I wanted to examine the other side – the key traits of mental wellness. So, I, along with a colleague who has worked as a coach and mentor to women, decided to write this book for women so they can be their healthiest and take the necessary steps to live a life that is as vibrant and vital as possible.

My colleague and I decided to ask women, lots of women just like you, what mental wellness characteristics or traits they thought best described Today's Healthy Woman. Here's what they came up with:

Humorous
Confident
Loving
Spiritual
Balanced
Optimistic
Self-accepting
Fit
Self-nurturing
Passionate

These are the ten key traits of Today's Healthy Woman. Now that you know what they are, the next step is to begin making each one an integral and vital part of your life. And that's what this book will help you do – master these ten traits through our "Ten-Week Take Back Your Life Program." It's fun, guilt-free (that's our goal when you complete the program) and a sure-fire way to truly enjoy your life.

Keep in mind that we also have a website **www.healthyinspiration.com** where you will find additional strategies and support as you work toward being the healthiest woman you know! We'd also like to hear from you on your journey towards a healthier you!!

Good health and happiness!

Barbara McFarland, EdD
Psychologist

Steve Wuest
Consultant, Coach and Mentor

The Take Back Your Life Program

Taking back your life simply means that you will make yourself a priority. You have to really understand and know that if you don't take care of yourself, no one around you will thrive or be happy. Many of the teen-age girls brought to therapy by their parents because of eating disorders, poor grades, and attitude problems often get better when I start meeting with their moms. I soon discover that many of these moms are stressed out, overwhelmed and generally put everyone else's needs first. My favorite teaching adage is, "When mommy's happy, everyone's happy." So, I counsel them to take better care of themselves and to make some time for themselves. It's quite uncanny, but as soon as mom begins focusing on her own unmet needs, the kids improve. I hope I've made my case!

In ten week's time, you will be a living, breathing example of Today's Healthy Woman. Your daughters, sisters, nieces, mothers, and any other significant female in your life, will not only notice a difference in you from the way you walk, smile, and act but they will also look to you as a role model for themselves. Much like the character in the Viagra commercial, everyone will want to know what's different about you! All you have to do is be willing to commit to take anywhere from 5 to 60 minutes a day implementing various aspects of the program. It works if you work it!

If you're thinking, "Where am I going to find even FIVE minutes for myself?" I'll tell you what I tell all of my patients who respond similarly. *We all make time for what we value most.* Just make up your mind to change that negative pattern of thinking. So, start putting yourself at the top of your list. No more excuses!

Getting Started

You will need a journal and pads of post-it notes as you go through this program. We've placed a Journal page at the end of each chapter and some more at the end of the book. You may want to buy a separate one. Do what works best for you. We'd also strongly suggest that you have a *Today's Healthy Woman Poster* displayed in a visible place as well as *The Today's Healthy Woman Tip Sheet* (available at **www.healthyinspiration.com**). These tools will keep you on track. Let me tell you why they are an essential aspect of this program.

Cues For Success

No one can deny that you're hounded by the demands of your multiple roles and responsibilities and caught between competing priorities of home, family, and the workplace, leaving little, if any time, to take care of yourself. That's a reality.

Here's another reality. There are hundreds of articles, books, TV shows, websites and pamphlets promoting self-care for women. You, like most other women I know, have become hypnotized by these self-help gurus and their prescriptions for good health and well-being. You hear the message, nod your head and say, "Yes, that's just what I need to do." However, like most women, you're probably not actually DOING what is suggested to improve your physical and emotional health on a consistent basis. Part of the problem is time. I say that's remedied by re-evaluating priorities. The other part of the problem is that you simply forget or procrastinate. So, how can you *remember* to take care of yourself and find the time to do so?

In trying to help people change patterns of thinking or behavior, psychologists have encouraged people to use "cues" to help them make the desired behavior change. For example, people can set their wrist watches to beep as a reminder to exercise or to take medication. Fitness programs often encourage the use of a "buddy" and weight loss programs sometimes use weekly weigh-ins and discussions. All of these are cues intended to keep the individual focused on the goal.

The poster and tip sheet can serve as this "cue" for you since they can be displayed in the most common areas of your environment. (I have my poster displayed in my kitchen. Every time I walk out the door I am reminded to work on a trait. Other women I know have placed it on closet doors, in laundry rooms, exercise rooms, or office cubicles.) Well, that's what makes this program so unique. We're not going to let you forget! These tools are the cues that will help you succeed in taking your life back and mastering the traits.

As for the time crunch—this program is designed to fit INTO your life so that it will be less of a struggle to focus on yourself and do the things you choose to do.

Should Do's And Want To's

One last thing we have to address before you get started. Take a few minutes and write down in the space below the things or activities you feel you SHOULD DO and the things or activities you feel you WANT TO DO.

SHOULD DO'S	WANT TO DO'S
————————	————————
————————	————————
————————	————————

My guess is your "Should Do" list includes things or activities that are responsibilities and tasks that you need to do for others or some unpleasant task you might need to do for yourself, "I should exercise." Or "I should eat healthier." "I should be nicer to my hubby." Your "Want to Do" list might include activities or things that are fun and relaxing and, in some cases, perhaps not so good for you as well. For example, "I want to eat a gallon of ice-cream." Or "I want to take a week-end trip."

As you begin this program, we expect that the majority of strategies you choose will at first be "SHOULD DO's." Anytime people attempt to change behaviors and attitudes, their initial mindset is a "SHOULD DO" one. "I should exercise for 20 minutes each day." "I should eat more fruits and vegetables." If they hang in there and persist, an amazing thing happens—their attitude catches up to their behavior and shifts to a "WANT TO DO." "I want to exercise for 20 minutes each day." "I want to eat more fruits and vegetables." Famed psychiatrist William Glasser wrote a book on this phenomenon called, *Positive Addiction.*

Our hope is that you will make taking care of yourself a positive addiction. Be patient and persistent. If you work this program, it will work for you!!

The Take Back Your Life Program

Unlike other programs, this program doesn't tell you what to do or when to do it. You're in control with some minimal guidance. What's really great about this program is that YOU customize it. Here's how you begin.

First identify which of the ten traits you'll work on each week for ten weeks. You might want to begin by choosing the easier ones—those that you feel you have a head start on. Or you may want to begin with the more challenging ones—those that you know are missing from your life.

Write one of the ten traits for each week in the space below – the ten traits are Balanced, Self-Nurturing, Humorous, Self-Accepting, Optimistic, Spiritual, Self-Nurturing, Confident, Fit, and Passionate.

THE TAKE BACK YOUR LIFE PROGRAM

WEEK ONE_____ WEEK SIX_____
WEEK TWO_____ WEEK SEVEN_____
WEEK THREE_____ WEEK EIGHT_____
WEEK FOUR_____ WEEK NINE_____
WEEK FIVE_____ WEEK TEN_____

Although nothing is cast in stone, do try and commit to each of these as you've listed them above without changing them during the ten-week period.

In a calendar or in your daily planner, write each trait down on the first day of the week for the next ten weeks in these words: *I am Balanced, I am Humorous, I am Self-nurturing, etc.*

This strategy is critical in that it re-enforces your commitment to the program. It would also help if you would verbally share your weekly traits with someone you trust. So, you've chosen, written and shared your program. You're on your way!

Three Steps to Mastery/Program Overview

Now that you have your program mapped out, you will basically complete three relatively easy steps in each chapter to achieve mastery of each trait. Since living these traits is an ongoing process, *we define mastery as having accomplished the weekly goals you established for yourself.* Below is an example of how you would follow these three easy steps in each chapter.

> **Step One - Read, Rate and Reflect on your Trait-of-the-Week**

On the first day of the week, take 15-20 minutes and read about the trait you chose, complete the quiz and the self-rating scale. If you wish, write any strong feelings

TAKE BACK YOUR LIFE NOW!

or reactions you have about your self-rating or about anything you've read in that particular chapter. We'd also suggest that you write your weekly trait on some post-it notes in this way, "I AM (TRAIT)" and plaster them around the house – on your bathroom mirror, car visor, refrigerator door, cubicle wall. Having reminders in key spots will keep you focused on your weekly trait. As the week wears on, don't let the post-it notes fade out. Every day make sure they are visible and sticking!

> **Step Two - Choose and Commit to your Trait-of-the-Week**

When you get to the section entitled *How Can I Be a Ten?*, read the strategies presented and choose one or two for the week or come up with one of your own. Look at your planner or calendar and consider all that you have going on. Be sure to choose a strategy or create one of your own that you are most likely to actually implement. We developed strategies that take anywhere from 5 to 60 minutes. The goal is to make sure you actually *live* this trait in some way shape or form every single day.

In your daily planner or your calendar, schedule this strategy just as you would schedule anything else. For example, in the *I am Humorous* chapter, one of the strategies is to choose someone in your network of family or friends who is the most fun loving and upbeat. Schedule to spend some time with this person – meet for coffee or breakfast, or just call him or her on the phone. But schedule it in and make it happen!

Depending on the strategy, you may schedule the activity three or more times a week. Another strategy in the Humorous chapter is to tell a joke a day. Well, write that strategy in your planner for each day of the week.

At this time, choose a reward you will give yourself if you keep your trait-of-the-week commitments. It can be a manicure, pedicure, massage or facial—or you can ask your partner for a back-rub, do your own nails or buy a new lipstick. Write your reward down in your journal.

> **Step Three - Review and Reward**

On the last day of the week, find 10 or 15 minutes to sit down and review your progress for the week. Take out your calendar or planner and evaluate how you did in living your trait of the week. In your journal, rate yourself on a 1-10 scale—with one being "I didn't do anything" and 10 being "I mastered the trait." We emphasize that mastery means that you made the time each day to raise your awareness about your attitude and behaviors in living the trait and that you dutifully completed every strategy you wrote in your planner. Remember – progress NOT perfection! In your journal, reflect on what it was like to live this trait by asking yourself some reflective questions like these:

- How did it make a difference in my day-to-day routine? Energy level?
- What do I think others noticed different about me when I emulated the trait?
- How do I feel about myself when I emulate this trait?

If you rated yourself a 7 or better, you get your reward that you identified on Day One. Then, go back to Step One and select another trait for the upcoming week.

We just gave you an overview of the three-step process so don't worry about remembering all of this. We'll guide you along the way as you go through the book so, relax and enjoy.

Here's to taking your life back!

I AM BALANCED

It's important to remember that there is a difference between a balanced life and a balancing act.
Anonymous

> **Step 1** — **Read, rate and reflect.**
> *Take 15 to 20 minutes on the first day of the week to complete this step.*

A balanced life, yeah right. How does that fit with the juggling act you usually perform? We all yearn for and talk about being balanced but we usually feel powerless to achieve it. Collapsing into bed after a day overflowing with work deadlines, cooking, cleaning and shuttling kids from soccer to piano, do you sometimes think, just before sinking into much needed sleep, "How wonderful it would be to have a more balanced life?"

Is that really possible without sending the kids off to an orphanage, putting your husband on a once a year visitation schedule and burning your never ending to do list? So where do you start?

First a more balanced life means different things to different people. For Oprah it might mean she has clean towels in every bathroom in all of her nine homes. For Raymond's wife, Deborah, it might be an hour away from her mother-in-law, kids, and her much loved husband. So, what's balance for you? Generally, a balanced woman feels in control, has a realistic sense of what she can and cannot accomplish and is flexible in her daily routines. She's more focused on doing what she needs to do for herself, her work life and her family as opposed to measuring up to some idealized standard.

Where does Balance Begin?

First, let's look at the number of balls a woman has to juggle on any given day:

- Personal needs
- Relationships, including immediate and extended family, friends, co-workers, and neighbors
- Life work
- Spirituality
- Health
- Finances
- Recreation and leisure activities

As we move through life, our focus is always changing and our juggling is never easy or finished. As a new mother, children take priority, but as time and situations change, our career or health may require more of our time and focus.

Achieving a balanced life means becoming aware of what balance is for you and then making decisions to move toward change. Knowing what balance feels like for you helps you become more sensitive or aware of your "out-of-balance" symptoms. For many these include headaches, muscle aches, mood swings, or irritability. Use these signs to measure and nurture your balance quotient. Remember, a Balanced Woman accepts that she can't do everything!

If you feel out of balance, don't fret. Knowing that you're out of balance is the first major step to reaching balance. Take time to sort out what's important to YOU and get comfortable with your new perspective. Be prepared for some resistance from your family and friends. After all, they're used to you picking up the slack.

The Healthy Woman Self-Rating Scale

Now let's get more specific in this area of balance. On our *Healthy Woman Self-Rating Scale* with 10 being "I'm Olympic Material" and 1 being "I need more training!" circle where you would rate your balance level today.

*TAKE BACK YOUR LIFE **NOW!***

I need more training　　　　**I'm Olympic Material**

Now, let's do a reality check and see how accurate your self-rating is. Write "yes" or "no" to the questions below. Remember, no cheating and there are no right or wrong answers.

- Am I satisfied with my home and family life? (or would I rather move and leave no forwarding address?)
- Is my home and family life what I thought it would be? (…happily ever after or dysfunction junction?)
- Do I have interests outside my career and family?
- Do I have friends that enrich my life?
- Do I take time for myself? (going to the bathroom does not count!)
- Do I get regular health check-ups? (The blood pressure machine at the pharmacy doesn't count.)
- Do I enjoy my current lifework situation?
- Am I comfortable with my financial habits?
- Do I say "yes" to myself as much as I do to everyone else?
- Can I say "No" to others when it would be in my best interest to do so?

If you answered "yes" to the majority of these questions, you're in great shape and should have rated

I AM BALANCED

yourself a 7 or above on the self-rating scale. If not, read on!

Let's get a little more specific on the balance trait. On a scale of 1 to 10, with ten being very balanced and 1 being not at all, rate yourself in the following areas:

- ☐ Self   _____
- ☐ Family   _____
- ☐ Friendships   _____
- ☐ Career/lifework _____
- ☐ Spirituality   _____
- ☐ Health   _____
- ☐ Financial   _____
- ☐ Recreation   _____

Total   _____

A score of 70 or above is awesome. You go girl! A score of 50 is ok. You need some work. A score of 40 or below says you will greatly benefit by embracing everything this book has to offer!! (Keep your score and check back later, say in six months, to see how you're changing and how you're doing on your goal.)

As you look at your score, where are you in good shape? What do you need to keep doing? Where do you need to make improvements?

In your journal or on the journal page at the end of this chapter, choose only one area that you would like to work on and set a realistic, achievable goal for change.

DID YOU KNOW...

It was once thought that multiple roles (employee, mother, wife, daughter-in-law, etc.) and their balancing caused stress. However, research shows that multiple roles actually have beneficial outcomes. These include added income, social support, and opportunities to experience success, perspective and what they call buffering.

Buffering is an interaction between two roles that helps the successes in one role offset the failures in another. For example, if there was turmoil at home but yet you got a promotion at work, the stress at home might be tempered by your success at work. So, keeping your roles balanced will insure your overall well-being. High levels of role satisfaction were associated with low levels of depression and anxiety.

I AM BALANCED

Step 2   **Choose and Commit**
Now choose one of the following strategies or create one of your own for the upcoming week and schedule it in your planner. Be sure to choose a reward for yourself.

So, How Can I Be a Ten?

Living a balanced life takes constant attention to what is important to you and to what you are doing. You must be a good communicator and be willing to change as needed. The payoff for the effort will be worth it.

Strategy #1- Walk down Memory Lane
15 minutes

Think back over the last five years and remember when you felt a high degree of balance versus when you felt out of balance.

In your own journal or on the journal page at the end of this chapter, draw a timeline representing the past five years. Now identify the times during those five years when you felt more in control or had a high degree of balance in your life. Write those down above the line.

Now think of the times when you felt out of balance, off kilter, or out of control. Write those down below the line.

Consider these questions: what was it about each period that created balance or imbalance? What was different in your life? How were YOU different? What were you DOING? What have you learned from these periods about how to maintain a greater level of balance?

In your planner or calendar, write down one thing or two things you can do this week to begin achieving balance. Schedule them in.

Strategy # 2 – Create A Vision
20 minutes

There are two tasks to this strategy. First, ask yourself, "What do I want to feel, do, own, and contribute in life?" In your journal or on the journal page at the end of this chapter, make a list that is tangible, measurable, and within set time periods. We suggest updating your vision every year. For example:

- Do – I want to begin taking evening classes at the local college. Or, I want to get a new job where I can work with people.

I AM BALANCED

- Own – I want to put a down payment on that house I always dreamed about. Or, I want to buy home exercise equipment to make it easier to get in shape.
- Contribute – I want to volunteer my time at a hospital or community agency. Or, I want to serve on a committee for a local charity.
- Feel – I want to nurture new friendships with Mary and Elizabeth in my personal life. Or, I want to feel close to my daughter by being more involved in her school activities.

Task Two
30 –45 minutes

Step two is a whole lot of fun you can either do by yourself or invite a close girlfriend to make a night of it with you. It will require some time however. Make a collage and this will re-enforce your vision statement. Lock yourself in a room where you can't be disturbed. Put a sign on the door that says "DO NOT DISTURB OR YOU'LL BE SORRY!! Get a glass of wine, put on your favorite music, or do whatever relaxes you, and gather some old magazines. Tear out magazine photos or words that speak to you about your goals.

Review your vision statement and the steps you decided to take in order to reach your goals. Paste your clippings together on a paper or a piece of poster board. Be creative! Hang the artistic version of your Vision where you will be reminded of it everyday—maybe on your closet door or in your cubicle at work. Hang it on the refrigerator and let your family see what is important to YOU!!

Remember, what you can see clearly, you can do. Schedule this strategy in your planner.

Strategy # 3 – Priority Check
15 Minutes

There are 168 hours in a week. How do you spend yours?

Sleeping _____
Leisure_____
Eating_____
Commuting_____
Household chores____
Cooking_____
Working _____
Shopping_____
Other_____
Time with family_____
Time for self_____

As you look at your allocations, what do you need to do differently to have more balance in your day?

Focus on one area and establish what you will do differently for the upcoming week. Some examples might be:
- I will get to bed by 10:00 so that I have at least 7 hours sleep each night.
- I will read a story to my children three evenings this week.

Remember to schedule these into your planner.

Step 3 — **Review and Reward**

Do this on the last day of the week and be sure to reward yourself if you have succeeded.

In your journal review your progress for the week and then rate yourself:

Didn't do anything   Mastery

1............................5................................10

Ask yourself some reflective questions such as:

- How did working on this trait make a difference in my day-to-day routine? Energy level? Relationships?
- What do I think others noticed different about me when I emulated the trait?
- How do I feel about myself when I emulate this trait?

If you rated yourself a 7 or better, you get your reward that you identified on Day One. If you didn't, don't give up. Reassess what your biggest obstacle was and make a plan to deal with it more effectively. You might want to move onto another trait and come back to this one later. Whatever you do, don't give up.

TAKE BACK YOUR LIFE NOW!

THE HEALTHY WOMAN JOURNAL

I am Balanced

No matter how big or soft or warm your bed is, you still have to get out of it.
Grace Slick

I AM CONFIDENT

*If you really want something,
you can figure out how to make it happen.
Cher*

> **Step 1** — **Read, rate and reflect.**
> *Take 15 to 20 minutes on the first day of the week to complete this step.*

Are you Anna Freud or Edith Bunker? Freud's daughter once said, "I was always looking outside myself for strength and confidence but it comes from within. It is there all the time." We doubt Archie's wife would agree. She was always waiting for her beloved hubby to tell her what to do and what to think.

Where does confidence come from? Believe it or not you already have it. You just need to start using it! It's really a state of mind. Think of Jackie Kennedy, a woman who lived on her own terms. She remained in control and confident in herself and in her ability to handle whatever life dealt her. She believed in herself.

Having confidence is a very empowering, influential and contagious feeling. If you are confident you will address all those aspects of your life that are most important to you. Not only will you succeed most of the time, but you will also be able to bounce back when you face defeat. You will have the capability to influence all those around you, including family, friends, and co-workers. And by being confident, you will make those around you more confident as well. If everyone around you was as confident as you, how much do you think you could accomplish then? The sky would be the limit!

What's the Difference Between Someone Who is Confident and Someone Who isn't?

Confident women have an attitude that focuses on the positive. They understand their strengths, have a general sense of control, and trust their abilities. As a result, they generally believe they can accomplish anything they set out to, within limits. Their expectations are realistic, and they are not devastated if their expectations are not always met.

People who lack confidence tend to look outside of themselves for approval and support. Remember Edith? Constant feedback and acceptance are too important to them. Because they lack confidence, they often fail to pursue the things most important to them for fear of failure. They are not risk takers. Confidence is not about having a perfect life but about dealing with the imperfections.

Why do Women Lose Confidence?

Many women adopt self-defeating ways of looking at things. Did you ever know a perfectionist? Or are you one? Are you a total failure or a total mess? It's not about absolutes. That reflects "all or nothing thinking" that can quickly erode your confidence. What really matters – that your napkins match the tablecloth? Or that you're having a take-out meal with people you care about? Do you know any "perfect" people who are fun anyway?

Some women accentuate the negative, and minimize the positive. Did you ever prepare a holiday dinner for your family and everyone just raved about everything but you knew that the hand sculpted butter pats were too hard? Can you ever forgive yourself? If your answer is no, you are eroding your confidence.

You may also lose confidence if you're too concerned about meeting other's expectations and you

TAKE BACK YOUR LIFE NOW!

always do what you believe you <u>should </u>do to meet those expectations. Eleanor Roosevelt once said, "No one can make you feel inferior without your consent." That is what confidence is all about. Trust yourself and your abilities. Remember, opinions are only opinions and yours are the most important.

<u>The Healthy Woman Self-Rating Scale</u>

On the Healthy Woman Rating Scale, circle where you would rate your confidence level today.

I don't know if I can…   **Bring it on!!!**

Let's do a reality check on your confidence levels. Write yes or no to the questions below.

- Do I feel capable of accomplishing my most important goals?
- Can I honestly accept compliments? (Oh, this old thing?)
- Is my self-talk positive and self-enhancing? (I think I can…I think I can.)
- Do I believe I can do most anything I set my mind to do?
- Do I walk proudly, give eye contact and speak in a confident, assertive tone of voice? (I am woman. Hear me roar!!!)

- Do I have a realistic sense of what I can and cannot do?
- Do I think I'm as smart, confident and attractive as most anybody else?
- Do I make the majority of my decisions based on what I think is best and not what others think? (The opinions of mother-in-laws don't count.)

If you answered "yes" to the majority of these questions, your self-rating should be at a 7 or above. If not, a few small changes can help quite a bit.

TAKE BACK YOUR LIFE NOW!

> **Step 2**   **Choose and Commit**
> *Choose one of the following strategies or create one of your own for the upcoming week and schedule it in your planner. Be sure to choose a reward.*

So, How Can I Be a Ten?

     Having confidence takes work and most of it has to do with your internal dialogues or self-talk messages. Pay attention to the kinds of thoughts you harbor about yourself or what you do. Replace the negative ones with more positive supportive messages. Be your own cheerleader!

I AM CONFIDENT

Another way to build confidence is to start by taking very small risks and working yourself up to the big ones! If you want to go back to school to get or finish your degree, start by taking just one class you know you could succeed in.

Strategy #1 – Develop The Full Glass Syndrome
10 Minutes

Give yourself credit whenever possible. Look in the mirror, into your eyes and say, "Job well done!" Pay attention to your *effort* when taking a risk and not always on the *outcome*. This is one place where "trying" does count! For example, instead of berating yourself for getting a "C" in a class or not getting the promotion you had hoped for, focus on your efforts or on the fact that you took the risk, be proud of yourself that you at least tried. Look at what didn't work and focus on changing that for the future. Make a realistic plan on how to achieve your goal. Reflect on the things you can do well, not on the things you struggle with.

In your journal or on the journal page at the end of this chapter, make a list of three things you have done well in the last three weeks and how each has benefited you. It doesn't matter how big or small.

Record any risks you may have taken over these past weeks. For example, if you ordered your steak medium and it comes back mooing, did you send it back? Look for the small attempts and remember the old saying, "A journey of a thousand miles begins with the first step."

What risk taking behavior can you schedule into your planner or calendar? An example might be, "Be assertive with my co-worker when she takes things from my desk." "Be assertive when my mom calls and asks when I'm coming over."

Strategy # 2 – Walk on the Wild Side
15 minutes

Ok, no more dilly-dallying. You just have to go for it and take a risk.

It helps to approach new experiences as *new opportunities to learn* rather than *fear them as chances to fail.* Again, try to get a healthy perspective on your risk-taking. Don't dwell on whether or not you'll fail or succeed or on what people will think of you. Focus more on the adventure of trying! Lighten up on yourself.

In your journal or on the journal page at the end of this chapter, identify one activity that you have avoided for fear of failure or of what others will think of you. See if you can break this activity into smaller steps so you're not overwhelmed by the desired outcome.

There was one woman I counseled who was incredibly talented at making jewelry. Her lack of confidence prohibited her from believing that anyone would ever buy her pieces. After some support, she agreed to have a small jewelry party at a friend's house to see if there was any interest in her work. Her jewelry brought in over $1,300.00 that evening. That whole experience boosted her confidence significantly. So much so that she approached a retailer who bought some more!!

Develop a plan of action, a timeline, and set goals. Choose someone that you've seen take risks, and tell her what your plan is. This will help you with your follow-through. Identify what steps you can take this week toward your goal and schedule them in your planner or calendar. There is no greater "high" than being able to stand up to your fears and not let them control you!

Strategy # 3 – Fake it 'til you Make it!
10 Minutes

Look around and choose at least three women who exhibit the confidence levels that you desire. What do you observe about them? What characteristics do they seem to possess? How do they handle themselves?

Now choose one of these women. Select one trait of hers that you would like to emulate. Write it down in your journal or on the journal page at the end of this chapter and establish a goal for making that trait a part of your new confident self. Write your goal down on each day of the week in your planner. An example might be, "I'll walk with erect posture and a confident smile." Every time you refer to your planner, you will be reminded to act on your goal.

Step 3   <u>**Review and Reward**</u>
Do this on the last day of the week and be sure to reward yourself if you have succeeded.

In your journal review your progress for the week and then rate yourself:

Didn't do anything   Mastery

1................................5..................................10

Ask yourself some reflective questions such as:

- How did working on this trait make a difference in my day-to-day routine? Energy level? Relationships?
- What do I think others noticed different about me when I emulated the trait?
- How do I feel about myself when I emulate this trait?

If you rated yourself a 7 or better, you get your reward that you identified on Day One. If you didn't, don't give up. Reassess what your biggest obstacle was and make a plan to deal with it more effectively. You might want to move onto another trait and come back to this one later. Whatever you do, don't give up.

I AM CONFIDENT

THE HEALTHY WOMAN JOURNAL

I am Confident

I believe you rarely achieve more than you expect
Carol Grosse

_____
_____
_____
_____
_____
_____
_____
_____
_____

TAKE BACK YOUR LIFE NOW!

THE HEALTHY WOMAN JOURNAL

_____
_____
_____
_____
_____
_____
_____
_____
_____
_____
_____

I AM FIT

Fitness: If it came in a bottle,
everybody would have a good body.
Cher

TAKE BACK YOUR LIFE NOW!

> **Step 1**   **<u>Read, rate and reflect.</u>**
> *Take 15 to 20 minutes on the first day of the week to complete this step.*

"I know I SHOULD exercise, but I just don't have the time." "I'm intimidated by the idea that I have to do strength training and then aerobics. Forget it."

Sound familiar? Well, the good news is that research shows ANY movement is better than none when it comes to being fit. Take the stairs, walk the dog, park your car a ways from your destination, and LAUGH MORE! See how good that feels.

DID YOU KNOW…

Laughing increases muscular and respiratory activity, and stimulates the cardio-vascular system. After your next real belly laugh, place your hand over your heart and feel your accelerated heart beat. It will continue to be elevated for up to 5 minutes. Laughter also, increases antibodies and decreases stress hormones. Think of laughing as the jogging of the internal organs! And then there's SEX!! Yes, having sex boosts the immune system, strengthens the heart and diminishes arthritis.

So, being fit doesn't mean pain and dread. Be creative! Turn household drudgery into fun! Put on something with a good beat and vacuum away. It worked for Melanie Griffith in Working Girl! Just move your body around and give it some form of exercise at least 35-40 minutes three times a week. As for the dirty DIET word - look at portion sizes, fat content, and patterns of eating. It's not what you eat; it's how much you eat!

Don't make being fit and eating healthy more difficult than it needs to be. SOMETHING IS BETTER THAN NOTHING. Ask yourself what kind of shape do you want to be in when you're 40, 50, or even 75?

DID YOU KNOW...

The leading cause of death among women? If you said breast cancer you're WRONG! It's cardiovascular disease – one death every 33 seconds! So start moving!!

So, Why is Fitness so Important?

Instead of talking about the importance of fitness from the usual medical standpoint, let's talk about it from the standpoint of the traits in this book.

First, today's healthy woman has balance in her life. She balances family, relationships, her needs, a career, the financial aspects of her life, leisure time and her spiritual life. Seldom does a woman feel like she has excess time to get everything done. Instead, she feels like she has to be Superwoman. Therefore, the energy and sense of well being that is gained from some form of exercise and healthy eating is vital to her being able to balance her life.

Mild depression is offset by increased exercise which stimulates endorphins. These are the naturally feel good chemicals in the brain that keep you motivated, optimistic and moving in the right direction.

Second, do you think a woman is likely to be confident and optimistic if she is drastically overweight, has trouble walking up a flight of stairs, or has a serious illness? Not likely. Good fitness facilitates being confident and optimistic.

What about being a loving woman? It takes a lot of energy for all the family, friends, and relationships that you

TAKE BACK YOUR LIFE NOW!

have in your life. A good fitness and nutrition level is paramount to having a great capacity for love.

Good mental fitness is key to finding your spiritual self and finding that centeredness and grounding that we all want. We could go on, but it's clear that without fitness and overall health, it will be difficult to achieve high levels of health in the other traits that describe today's healthy woman.

The Healthy Woman Self-Rating Scale

On the Healthy Woman Rating Scale, circle where would you rate your fitness level today.

Certified couch potato   **Mover and shaker**

So, let's do a reality check on your self-rating. I'm sure you know some of these questions by heart but here they are anyway. In our experience, many women (and men, too!) tend to have this wonderful way of denying or minimizing just how much food they REALLY eat and how little exercise they get.

I AM FIT

- Do I drink plenty of fluids?
- Do I make fairly healthy food choices? (Chocolate isn't a food group.)
- Is my energy level sufficient to do everything I want to do?
- Do I get some form of exercise several times a week? (taking the stairs every day or parking farther away than necessary from your destination, etc.).
- Can I walk two flights of stairs without being winded? (Ten-minute rest stops on the landing don't count.)
- Do I use alcohol in moderation?
- Have I stopped smoking yet? (No, what would I do for a New Year's Resolution then?)
- Do I get enough sleep?
- Do I get preventive screenings on a regular basis or as my physician recommends such as mammograms, pap smears, and colonoscopies? (Do I schedule, cancel, re-schedule?)

A yes to these questions puts you at a TEN on our Healthy Woman Rating Arrow. Congrats and keep up the good work. Couch Potatoes can turn into Movers and Shakers with a few small changes.

You can use the rating arrow above as a way to set some goals for yourself. If you rated yourself at a 3.5, what is <u>one small step</u> you can take to move up to a 4? Would it be to limit your fast food intake to one time a week? Or might it be to use low fat salad dressings or sugar free soft drinks for one week? Keep it small and achievable.

Step 2	**<u>Choose and Commit</u>**
	Choose one of the following strategies or create one of your own for the upcoming week and schedule it in your planner. Be sure to choose a reward.

So, How Can I Be a Ten?

Being fit takes work, commitment and most of all positive self-coaching. You can start by taking small steps – take the stairs instead of the elevator, choose low fat dressing instead of regular, eat less red meat and more fish and chicken. It doesn't have to be so PAINFUL!! Visualize yourself at 40, 50, or even 75. How do you want to feel and look at those times in your life?

Strategy #1 – Any movement is Good!
5-10 minutes

In your planner or calendar, schedule in one fitness and healthy eating goal for the week. This will help you move up that scale one number! For example, I will use the stairs instead of the elevator at work for the next week. I will eat one piece of fruit a day (not dipped in chocolate either). I will walk around the neighborhood three times this week (this one may even help some of your social goals). If you have a dog, she'll be grateful. If you don't, borrow one from a neighbor. Go a little easy on yourself but definitely stretch yourself. Recruit a buddy to keep you on track. At the end of the week, write in your journal how you did and how you feel.

One of my patients, whom I'll call Mary Beth, wanted to lose weight and after much discussion agreed to replace her daily 6 can addictive dose of regular coke with diet coke. That was her one and only goal for 6 weeks. She lost 4 ½ lbs. Interestingly enough she serendipitously discovered that she had a whole lot more energy. Eventually, she replaced her diet cokes with water.

Strategy #2 – Fitness Buddy
15 minutes

Find a friend that has the same desire to improve her fitness as you do. Get together and map out a plan. Set goals for fitness routines (i.e. Walk three time a week for 30 minutes) and levels (walk a mile in 15 minutes), nutrition habits (fast food only once a week, drink three bottles of

TAKE BACK YOUR LIFE NOW!

water a day), and other (low fat salad dressing, frozen yogurt instead of ice-cream). Workout together if possible. Research and plan healthy meals together. Check on each other everyday and reinforce good habits. Be committed to helping each other succeed. Celebrate with each other when you do reach milestones. And don't celebrate with a hot fudge sundae!

Strategy # 3 – Be a kid again
15 minutes

This strategy is for those of you who rated yourselves a 3 or less on the Healthy Woman Self-Rating Scale. Although this is really a fun one for anyone!

Think back to when you were 10, 11 and 12 years old. What physical activities did you enjoy doing? Skipping rope? Skating? Playing hopscotch? Tumbling? Wrestling with your siblings? Remember the Hokey-Pokey? Running to see how fast you could go? Bike riding? Well, brainstorm as many activities as you can remember and write them in your journal or on the journal page at the end of this chapter. If you're having trouble remembering, ask your mom or one of your siblings or childhood friends. Then, pick one and schedule this activity in your daily planner two times for the coming week. Once you get back in touch with how much fun it is and how good it feels to move that body of yours, you'll change your ways forever! Well, at least we hope so.

> **Step 3** **Review and Reward**
> Do this on the last day of the week and be sure to reward yourself if you have succeeded.

In your journal review your progress for the week and then rate yourself:

Didn't do anything   Mastery

1............................5................................10

Ask yourself some reflective questions such as:

- How did working on this trait make a difference in my day-to-day routine? Energy level? Relationships?
- What do I think others noticed different about me when I emulated the trait?
- How do I feel about myself when I emulate this trait?

If you rated yourself a 7 or better, you get your reward that you identified on Day One. If you didn't, don't give up. Reassess what your biggest obstacle was and make a plan to deal with it more effectively. You might want to move onto another trait and come back to this one later. Whatever you do, don't give up.

TAKE BACK YOUR LIFE NOW!

THE HEALTHY WOMAN JOURNAL

I am Fit

Supposing you have tried and failed again and again. You may have a fresh start any moment you choose, for this thing that we call "failure" is not the falling down but the staying down.
Mary Pickford

_____

_____

_____

_____

_____

_____

_____

_____

_____

I AM HUMOROUS
4

He who laughs, lasts.
Mary Poole

*TAKE BACK YOUR LIFE **NOW!***

Step 1	**<u>Read, rate and reflect.</u>**
	Take 15 to 20 minutes on the first day of the week to complete this step.

What makes Ethel and Lucy, Laverne and Shirley and the Golden Girls so well watched? Viewers could always count on a few belly laughs each episode as these women overcame their latest calamity. They taught us to laugh at ourselves and not be so serious about this thing called life.

Researchers have found that a good laugh can burn up as many calories per hour as a brisk walk. They also speculate that laughter triggers the release of endorphins, the brain's opiates. This may account for the pain relief that accompanies laughter. Norman Cousins claimed to nurse himself back to health from a crippling arthritic condition, in part, with old tapes of Candid Camera television programs and Marx Brothers movies.

One of my patients, Sue Ellen, was very distraught about the holidays. She was to have Christmas dinner at her home with her in-laws, which was becoming exceedingly stressful due to her sister-in-law's increasing dependence on drugs, which resulted in extremely unpredictable and volatile behavior. To add to her anxiety, her husband and his 3 brothers tended to be overtly hostile toward their sister, which created a most uncomfortable atmosphere for everyone. She sobbed as she explained this chaotic situation to me. "I feel so trapped. Everyone looks at me to take sides." Suddenly through her tears she began to smile. The smile turned into outright laughter. "I know what I'll do. I'm going to buy a Swiss flag and carry it around and whenever one of them wants me to take a side, I'll wave it and tell them I'm neutral, I'm neutral!" She did just that and told me afterwards that none of them could keep the negative momentum going. Every time she waved the flag, they couldn't help but laugh at themselves and the situation.

Humor helped her feel better and made her holiday a bit more bearable.

So, How Else Does Laughter Help?

Humor and laughter helps you manage your stress levels. When you laugh you are filled with light-hearted, cheerful, and upbeat feelings. It is hard to be stressed and negative with those feelings. When was the last time you had a good belly laugh? If it was when you were a kid, you are way behind.

DID YOU KNOW...

- *The average child laughs 150 times a day while an adult only laughs 15 times a day?*
- *Women profess to be slightly less fun-oriented than men, though most agree they are "a fun person to be around" (90%). But only half (50%) say they "live for having fun," and about four in ten (39%) agree that "having fun" is an over-rated concept.*
- *About three-quarters (73%) of women say they take time on at least a weekly basis to have fun, and they are most likely to say this between the ages of 18 and 34.*

Laughter engages people, helps form relationships, and maintains existing ones. As Victor Borge said "Laughter is the shortest distance between two people."

TAKE BACK YOUR LIFE NOW!

The Healthy Woman Self-Rating Scale

On the Healthy Woman Rating Scale, circle where you would rate your funny bone.

Sour puss **Life of the party**

So, let's do a reality check on your self-rating.

- Do I laugh so rarely that people would think I had a facelift if I did?
- Do I think pranksters and people who tell (clean) jokes are idiots?
- When I see people having fun or laughing do I think they're wasting time and should get back to work? (or do I wonder if they're laughing at me?)
- Do I hide when people play fun games at parties?
- Do I consider someone who reads the funnies in the newspaper severely intellectually impaired?
- Do I want to choke anyone who plays a practical joke on me?
- When I'm stressed out or faced with a difficult situation, it's especially uncomfortable for me to use humor as a coping mechanism?

I AM HUMOROUS

If you answered no to most of these questions, you're a fun person and probably get a lot of invitations to parties! Congrats Life of the party! If you answered yes to most of these questions, you need to get a grip and stop taking everything so seriously.

Step 2	**Choose and Commit**
	Choose one of the following strategies or create one of your own for the upcoming week and schedule it in your planner. Be sure to choose a reward.

So, How Can I Be a Ten?

We all know that you can't change a serious woman into Ms. Happy-Go-Lucky overnight. And we can't make ourselves laugh at a bad joke. So how do we expose ourselves to more humor? Here are a few tips.

Strategy #1 – Exercise your Funny Bone
45-60 minutes

Go to the video store and rent a comedy or watch the Comedy Channel on cable. Read a humorous book or read an appropriately funny book to your children. Schedule it in your planner or calendar.

45 minutes

Play a game with your family. One night a week, everyone is required to tell a joke at the dinner table. The person who gets the loudest laughs, wins a prize!

90 minutes

Go to a comedy club instead of out to dinner some weekend.

15 minutes

Take inventory of your network of family and friends. Who is the most fun loving and upbeat? Plan to spend more time with this person.

Since kids laugh 150 times a day, hang out with some kids! If you don't have a kid, borrow one. Go to a toy store, a park or even volunteer doing something that involves kids.

I AM HUMOROUS

Strategy # 2 – Create a Joke File
3 minutes

Have a joke file or write your own book of jokes. Make a habit of writing down funny things you hear or read. These may originate from TV, a movie, your friends, children, bumper stickers, and many other sources. You can do this in your journal. Choose one funny saying that you can repeat to yourself whenever you are stressed or angry.

Strategy # 3 – Laugh at Yourself
Any time

Don't take yourself so seriously. Ask yourself, how would Lucy handle this? Being able to laugh at yourself helps you to realize that your shortcomings don't really matter that much.

10 minutes

For one week, before you go to sleep, review your day and reflect on those times that you got angry or upset and could've laughed at yourself instead. Don't be critical of yourself while doing this exercise! Be a <u>Reflective Observer</u> and then identify what you will do differently the next time a similar situation arises. This is how you get better and better at being a more lighthearted and humorous person. In your journal or in the journal page at the end of this chapter, write down how you will handle similar situations in the future.

In the morning, take about 5 minutes and while looking at yourself in the mirror, make some really weird and funny faces. It would be fun to do this with your kids and a great way to get them out of bed!

Step 3 — Review and Reward

Do this on the last day of the week and be sure to reward yourself if you have succeeded.

In your journal review your progress for the week and then rate yourself:

Didn't do anything   Mastery

1............................5................................10

Ask yourself some reflective questions such as:

- How did working on this trait make a difference in my day-to-day routine? Energy level? Relationships?
- What do I think others noticed different about me when I emulated the trait?
- How do I feel about myself when I emulate this trait?

If you rated yourself a 7 or better, you get your reward that you identified on Day One. If you didn't, don't give up. Reassess what your biggest obstacle was and make a plan to deal with it more effectively. You might want to move onto another trait and come back to this one later. Whatever you do, don't give up.

I AM HUMOROUS

THE HEALTHY WOMAN JOURNAL

I am Humorous

The important thing in acting is to be able to laugh and cry. If I have to cry, I think of my sex life. If I have to laugh, I think of my sex life.
Glenda Jackson

TAKE BACK YOUR LIFE NOW!

<u>THE HEALTHY WOMAN JOURNAL</u>

I AM LOVING 5

We can only learn to love by loving.
Iris Murdoch

*TAKE BACK YOUR LIFE **NOW!***

> **Step 1** **Read, rate and reflect.**
> *Take 15 to 20 minutes on the first day of the week to complete this step.*

Name the loves in your life. Are you even on the list? Are you one of those women who think it's always better to give than to receive? Well, wake up! Now, it's your turn. And it's really ok, because if you don't receive, you'll have nothing to give.

Many women tend to see a loving woman as either the heroine in a romance novel or as Mother Teresa. There is a healthy achievable middle ground here.

In the romance novels, the woman never has to ask—her lover *always* knows what she wants, what she needs and what it takes to make her happy. You have to write your own story.

Here's where you start. You're in charge of what you get from others. But you have to first know what you want. Many women we've worked with really expect others to figure this out for them. Not their job.

It's fun to receive even if you've told people what you want and need. Most women initially recoil at the thought of actually telling someone what they want and need. "If I have to tell my partner what I want, it doesn't count." Think again.

A young mother of triplets sought counseling because she was quite depressed. For the past several weeks, she reported having sleepless nights, significant appetite changes and an overall feeling of despair. As she talked, it became clear that the onset of her depressed state started with the aftermath of Mother's Day.

She was so excited about her first mother's day that she couldn't sleep. She laid in bed imagining all these wonderful things her husband would do – maybe serve breakfast in bed, perhaps surprise her with a bouquet of flowers along with a homemade card from the kids.

Well, her husband actually forgot it was Mother's Day and when she made her way to the kitchen, he was on his way to a golf game. She was devastated but said nothing. Instead, she cried on and off throughout the day and had visions of wrapping a golf club around his neck upon his return. But, she didn't say or do anything for days and became increasingly depressed, feeling worthless and inadequate.

At our first session, she vacillated between sobbing and yelling about her husband. When I suggested she begin communicating more forthrightly about what she expects and needs, she shrunk back in horror. "I shouldn't have to do that. He should know. We've been married long enough." I asked her if her husband had psychic powers I wasn't aware of. She laughed and that's when she realized her expectations were way out of line.

On the following Mother's Day, she was served breakfast in bed along with a bouquet of flowers and a card from each of the triplets. How did that happen you ask? Well, one week before the big day, she explicitly told her husband what she expected and how he could show his appreciation. And she had a wonderful day!

You might say, well that was for a special event. What about the day-to-day stuff? It's really no different. You have to know what you want and then ask for it!

Learning to give and take is vital to healthy adult relationships. For health and ongoing satisfaction, make time everyday to pay attention to the reciprocity in your relationships. Think of it as a bank account. You have to make deposits to earn interest and have it when you need it. Constant withdrawals leave you bankrupt. Giving and taking on a daily basis helps keep love flowing in both directions.

TAKE BACK YOUR LIFE NOW!

DID YOU KNOW...

*More than 19 million Americans suffer from depression yearly and women are twice as likely as men to experience a major depressive episode. Depression may occur at any age during a woman's life with certain events like puberty, pregnancy, perimenopause, trauma, substance abuse and **quality of relationships** increasing the risk.*

*Current research has demonstrated that **relationships are more paramount to women's self-concept** than men and that women are more likely to experience stress in response to adverse events occurring in the lives of others and place their needs secondary to those of others.*

Thus, working at creating reciprocity and mutuality in your relationships can reduce feelings of depression.

<u>The Healthy Woman Self-Rating Scale</u>

On the Healthy Woman Rating Scale, circle where you would rate your lovingness level (as we describe it above) today.

1 2 3 4 5 6 7 8 9 10

All give no take　　　　　　**I know what I want and and I know how to ask**

So, let's do a reality check on your self-rating. Answer the following questions.

- Do I feel guilty when someone does something nice for me? (Is my first thought, "Oh no, what do I have to do for them now?")
- Is it difficult for me to be assertive when I think others are taking advantage of me?
- Do I go overboard in helping others and being there for others? (Keep in mind; there are no award ceremonies for Martyr of the Year.)
- Do I get angry when the people I give the most to, don't realize (mind read) when I need their help or assistance?

If you answered "yes" to most of these questions, you'll need to work on letting others give to you so you can move up the rating arrow. But remember, you have to communicate what it is you need.

TAKE BACK YOUR LIFE NOW!

> **Step 2**   **Choose and Commit**
> *Choose one of the following strategies or create one of your own for the upcoming week and schedule it in your planner. Be sure to choose a reward.*

So, How Can I Be a Ten?

Being a loving healthy woman will make your relationships more enjoyable and fulfilling. The key is to focus on the degree of reciprocity and mutuality that exist in each of your relationships.

Strategy #1 – Relationships Score Sheet
15 minutes

List all of your current relationships in the spaces below. Include, bosses, co-workers, neighbors, etc. Then rate how reciprocal and mutual each relationship is using a scale of 1 to 5 with five meaning the highest degree of reciprocity and mutuality and 1 being the very lowest. Be sure not to overanalyze! The purpose of this exercise is to give you a broad sense of the mutuality in your key relationships.

Remember, it's the little things that make a difference. Are you always the one who makes dinner reservations for the group? Do you always drive? Are you the one always waiting for everyone else? Are you always the hostess?

Name   **Rating**

- _____ 1...2...3...4...5
- _____ 1...2...3...4...5
- _____ 1...2...3...4...5
- _____ 1...2...3...4...5
- _____ 1...2...3...4...5
- _____ 1...2...3...4...5
- _____ 1...2...3...4...5

Do you see any patterns? Are they all near the 1 or 2 rank? See which relationships rank the highest and which the lowest. Then, in your journal or in the journal page at the end of this chapter, write down how you feel about these relationships. Indicate which ones you're ok with and which ones you would like to change. You might discover that it would be in your own best interests to "let go" of a relationship or minimize contact in a relationship that is not reciprocal and tends to take a lot out of you. Although difficult to do, a healthy woman is clear about where she wants to put her energy.

Strategy #2 – A "DO" Plan
15 minutes

Look at your inventory of relationships and make a plan as to how you can increase the reciprocity and mutuality in those relationships that rank a 1 or 2 or 3. But remember, you CANNOT control or change other people. Focus on what YOU can do differently to change the balance. Always ask yourself, "What can I do differently to make this relationship more reciprocal and mutual?"

One of the women I've worked with found that her least reciprocal relationship was with her mother. She had great difficulty saying "no" to her mom. One change she made was to "buy time" whenever her mother asked her to do something for her by saying, "Gee mom, let me get back to you on that. I'm not sure what else I have going that day." This allowed her to really think through whether or not she was able to or even wanted to do what her mom was asking of her. She planned an assertive response and found she was able to increase the reciprocity in that relationship.

Share your plan with a good friend whom you respect and see as someone who is able to receive and give in a more balanced way. Get feedback. Set a goal along with a deadline and then evaluate your progress. Remember again to focus on yourself and your actions.

Strategy #3 – Learning from Mistakes
15 minutes

I AM LOVING

For one week, before you go to sleep, review your day and reflect on those times that you could have been more assertive or forthcoming about what you needed from someone. Don't be critical of yourself while doing this exercise! You are to be a Reflective Observer and then identify what you will do differently the next time a similar situation arises. This is how you get better and better at being assertive and at handling conflict. In your journal or in the journal page at the end of this chapter, write down what you will do differently the next time a similar situation arises.

Develop assertiveness skills and conflict management skills. Look for classes in these topics at your local junior college or at the YWCA. Read some books on these topics, listen to tapes or watch videos.

Step 3 — **Review and Reward**

Do this on the last day of the week and be sure to reward yourself if you have succeeded.

In your journal review your progress for the week and then rate yourself:

Didn't do anything   Mastery

1................................5..................................10

*TAKE BACK YOUR LIFE **NOW!***

Ask yourself some reflective questions such as:

- How did working on this trait make a difference in my day-to-day routine? Energy level? Relationships?
- What do I think others noticed different about me when I emulated the trait?
- How do I feel about myself when I emulate this trait?

If you rated yourself a 7 or better, you get your reward that you identified on Day One. If you didn't, don't give up. Reassess what your biggest obstacle was and make a plan to deal with it more effectively. You might want to move onto another trait and come back to this one later. Whatever you do, don't give up.

I AM LOVING

THE HEALTHY WOMAN JOURNAL

I am Loving

I love people. I love my family, my children…but inside myself is a place where I live all alone and that's where you renew your springs that never dry up.
Pearl S. Buck

_____

_____

_____

_____

_____

_____

_____

_____

_____

TAKE BACK YOUR LIFE NOW!

THE HEALTHY WOMAN JOURNAL

_____

_____

_____

_____

_____

_____

_____

_____

_____

_____

_____

_____

_____

_____

I AM PASSIONATE

Don't be afraid that your life will end; be afraid that it will never begin.
Grace Hansen

TAKE BACK YOUR LIFE NOW!

> **Step 1**   **Read, rate and reflect.**
> *Take 15 to 20 minutes on the first day of the week to complete this step.*

What do you really, *really* care about? Is it at the top of your list? Or is it that thing you'll get around to when your day-to-day life is under control? Well, guess what. It's now or never. Someday is here!

What are you passionate about? And we don't mean chocolate, ice-cream, or gingerbread latte, even though they can do in a pinch.

Scores of women that I have worked with all have one thing in common. They don't know what being passionate means because they keep comparing themselves to people in popular culture who exude passion – Susan Sarandon, Candy Lightner (MADD founder), and Princess Diana.

Joan, a 39 year-old housewife I counseled, lamented that she had no talents and felt very "passion-less." Yet when she talked about upcoming holidays her descriptions of her preparations made Martha Stewart look like a slacker! As she talked about her handmade front door wreath to the snowflake embroidered hand towels in the guest bathroom, she became more and more animated. She WAS passionate but she didn't think that counted.

Passion doesn't have to be a national cause. Passion is what brings great energy to your life. Think about what makes you light up and get excited. It could be reading books to kids, baking cakes, organizing the cub scout fund drive or even caring for your pet.

Expand your definition of what passion is. You might not be seeing the passion in your life because like Joan, you don't see the value.

I AM PASSIONATE

Keep in mind that "passion" is not a fixed state but rather can change as your life circumstances change and as you age. The demands of a growing family along with a high-pressure job can leave little room for passionate pursuits. Depending upon your stage of life, family could very well BE your passion. As they grow and become more independent, you will need to expand your interests. It's easy to find passion in your life, if you just pay attention.

For some people work is their passion. As Confucius says, if you enjoy what you do, you'll never work a day in your life. Work that's perceived as drudgery or as meaningless will lead to depression, resentments, self-pity and anxiety. If you do anything with a "have to" attitude, your health will suffer.

DID YOU KNOW...

Women are most likely to be passionate about some kind of hobby or other activity (52%). Such passions grow steadily with age (e.g., 43% of 18-34 year-olds versus 64% of those 65-plus). But women are passionate about no one single hobby as much as they are about spending time with family—the most often mentioned passion (42%).

Women are not often able to indulge some of their passions. The majority does often get to spend time with their family (84%)—the most commonly cited activity they "love" to do—but only a minority often engages in other top passions, such as making love (34%) and spending a romantic evening with their spouse/partner (29%).

The Healthy Woman Self-Rating Scale

On the Healthy Woman Rating Scale below, circle where you would rate your passionate level today.

TAKE BACK YOUR LIFE NOW!

I just don't care   **I'm lovin' life**

So, let's do a reality check on your self-rating. Some women don't even know where to begin when it comes to this trait. Let's start with some questions to get you going:

- Do I feel a sense of energy, zest and excitement about some aspect of my life? (or is everyday as exciting as watching grass grow?)
- Do I generally feel that I'm doing what I was destined to do?
- Do I generally get out of bed looking forward to my day? (or is it just another rerun?)
- Am I able to have fun and laugh during my day?
- Do I feel as though my lifework is meaningful and makes a worthwhile contribution to my family and to the community? (or do I feel like no one would miss me?)
- Am I willing to take the risks necessary to discover what my passion might be?
- Do I have faith in myself that with some exploration I will be able to discover my passion?

If you answered yes to the questions, you're a passionate person or at least willing to do what's necessary to discover your passion. You should have rated yourself a 7 or above.

Step 2	**Choose and Commit**
	Choose one of the following strategies or create one of your own for the upcoming week and schedule it in your planner. Be sure to choose a reward.

So, How Can I Be a Ten?

Being passionate is a decision and takes effort like everything else worth having. It's knowing what you want, honoring your deepest desires and translating them into action. Connecting with your passionate side will only increase your energy, productivity and happiness. Being a ten on the passionate scale requires a major assessment of what turns you on. The key is to tune-in so you can be turned on!

Strategy #1 Putting Your Passionate Side to the Test
15 minutes

Using the self-rating scale, set some small goals. If you are a 1 or 2 on our Passionate scale, don't give up. Do an inventory of challenging and fun things you did as a kid up to adulthood. Make a list of these activities. Choose one that appeals to you and make a commitment to engage in that activity for the upcoming week and see what stirs within. If nothing comes to mind, then make a DREAM LIST of what you always wished you could do. Choose one of these dreams; pare it down so it's realistic and go for it.

Make a plan for change. Remember, we are trapped by our own self-limiting views of ourselves. Think BIG and GO FOR IT.

Some women we've worked with have had dreams of singing or playing the piano. Often these dreams are met with a judging mind that says, "You don't have any talent." Well, moving up the passionate scale requires that you tune out that negative thinking. Nothing is impossible. Taking those piano lessons or that art class can stimulate your passionate side.

Those of you at a 5, 6 or 7 on the passionate scale have the dreams but haven't acted upon them. These are the women who have made a thousand excuses for not pursuing what they are passionate about. You need to implement your dream one step at a time. This takes courage, conviction and patience! You can do it!! So go for it.

Roseann, a 45-year-old housewife, always dreamed of being a symphony pianist although realistically, her musical abilities were not at that level. So, she nurtured her dream by becoming a volunteer at the symphony,

I AM PASSIONATE

organizing children's groups to help ignite their interest in a life-long love of music.

Those of you at the upper end of the scale can't rest on your laurels. You have to keep your passionate side alive by nurturing it and exploring all sides of it. This is an ongoing process. Some women who have been passionate about raising their children must renew their passionate side once the kids leave home.

Strategy #2 – Live to the Fullest
every minute of your day

If it ain't broke, don't fix it! If you really enjoy what you do, enjoy it fully! Exude passion!! Verbalize your passion to those around you! Be contagious! Rub off on others.

10 minutes

At the end of each day, become the Reflective Observer and think about what was joyful or gratifying that particular day—what really turned you on.

Spend a few minutes reflecting on these pleasures and re-affirm your commitment to continue doing what is IMPORTANT TO YOU! Replace any negative self-talk with positive messages. Instead of, "I could never do that," think about what you need to know in order to begin taking small steps.

Until passion becomes second nature to you, you'll just have to make it happen. So, in your daily planner or in your journal, identify a specific pleasure and "schedule" it in as a weekly goal. For example a stay-at-home-mom who enjoys reading to her child(ren), can make that a goal for the week or if you are gratified by any aspect of your job, set up a meeting with your boss to discuss how you might make this a more regular part of your responsibilities.

TAKE BACK YOUR LIFE NOW!

You can increase these pleasures once you've plugged in to them. By increasing what's pleasurable to you, you will be in a better place to develop the passion within. You have to start somewhere.

Strategy #3– Passion Palette
In order to keep your passion burning and alive, you need to fuel it.

45-60 minutes

Focus on one of the pleasures you identified in Strategy #2. Grab some old magazines and start tearing out ideas or products that relate to your pleasure area. Let's say it was decorating. What could make that more fun for you? Do you need to learn more about color? Wall coverings? Accessorizing?

Organize what you found into piles that relate. Does one grouping excite you more than another? That's where you start. Back to our decorating example, if it's color, you could go to the library and get some books on color or check out your local university for adult education classes. Look in the newspaper for seminars led by local decorators.

There are lots of ways to feed your passion. You just have to be willing to spend some time discovering more about it.

Step 3	**Review and Reward**
	Do this on the last day of the week and be sure to reward yourself if you have succeeded.

In your journal review your progress for the week and then rate yourself:

Didn't do anything   Mastery

1............................5................................10

Ask yourself some reflective questions such as:

- How did working on this trait make a difference in my day-to-day routine? Energy level? Relationships?
- What do I think others noticed different about me when I emulated the trait?
- How do I feel about myself when I emulate this trait?

If you rated yourself a 7 or better, you get your reward that you identified on Day One. If you didn't, don't give up. Reassess what your biggest obstacle was and make a plan to deal with it more effectively. You might want to move onto another trait and come back to this one later. Whatever you do, don't give up.

TAKE BACK YOUR LIFE NOW!

THE HEALTHY WOMAN JOURNAL

I Am Passionate

Career is too pompous of a word. It was a job, and I have always felt privileged to be paid for what I loved doing.
Barbara Stanwyck

_____

_____

_____

_____

_____

_____

_____

_____

_____

I AM OPTIMISTIC 7

*Although the world is full of suffering,
it is full also of the overcoming of it.
Helen Keller*

> **Step 1** — **Read, rate and reflect.**
> *Take 15 to 20 minutes on the first day of the week to complete this step.*

How do you see a glass of water? This age old question is a quick and dirty method of determining whether or not you are an optimist (half-full) or a pessimist (half-empty). Your answer to this simple little quiz can tell you a lot about your ability to maintain good health.

DID YOU KNOW...

- *Optimists are more resistant to infectious illness and are better at fending off chronic diseases of middle age?*
- *People who learn to maintain an optimistic attitude may not only avoid depression but may also actually improve their physical health as* well?

So, your degree of optimism can play a key role in maintaining good emotional and physical health. And, people will like you a whole lot better, too!

So, What IS the Difference Between an Optimist and a Pessimist?

Optimists consistently overestimate their abilities. They tend to have a set of self-serving illusions that enable them to maintain good cheer and health. They persist in the face of insurmountable challenges and carry on when it is futile to do so - "I know I can beat this cancer."

Pessimists tend to explain adversity in permanent, pervasive and personal terms. They feel that no matter what

I AM OPTIMISTIC

they do, they cannot improve or affect the adverse situation in any way. They tend to personalize their problems and disappointments - "I wonder what I did wrong. How could I have cancer?"

Interestingly enough, pessimists are more reality-based than optimists! But, why take life so seriously? Optimists tend to have a veneer of denial when it comes to the harsher sides of life and always look to the "sunny side of the street."

Meet Kate, a 39-year-old attractive woman whose life looks a lot like most of ours. She had a 40-hour a week job, a husband and typical family responsibilities. Overnight her life changed. She was diagnosed with a brain tumor. Surgery left her with partial facial paralysis, deafness and visual impairment on one side.

When I first met her, I was taken off guard by her upbeat demeanor. I really expected her to have more issues regarding her physical disability; instead, she wanted to focus on a work-related issue. Was I surprised! Her first question to me was, "I've been given too much responsibility at work. I feel like I'm being taken advantage of. How do I set limits and start saying no?" And that's what we worked on.

As I got to know her, I became more and more intrigued about her coping skills related to the after effects of her surgery. When I asked her about this, she laughed. "You know. I don't think about it! This is life; at least this is my life. I'm just glad I'm alive."

I realized what made the difference for Kate was that she was able to focus on the big picture – her life was made up of many parts, some better than others. She never allowed herself to "get stuck" on any of her problems. She was truly an optimist.

The Healthy Woman Self-Rating Scale

On the Healthy Woman Rating Scale, circle where would you rate your optimism level today.

1 2 3 4 5 6 7 8 9 10

The sky is falling **Something great is right around the corner**

So, let's do a reality check on your self-rating. So, how optimistic are you *really?* Let's answer some questions:

- Do I tend to look at the bright side of things? (or am I constantly in the dark?)
- Even when given bad news, am I hopeful that a solution can be found?
- Do I tend to focus on the positives I have going for me and in my life? (or am I ready to trade places with my cat?)
- Am I proactive when it comes to my health, i.e., do I have mammograms, pap smears, colonoscopies, etc.
- Are my moods consistently pretty upbeat regardless of the weather, the kids' or the spouse?
- Do I sing or whistle for no reason at all? (or are they ready to vote me off the island?)

If you answered yes to the questions above, your glass is quite full!! Your self-rating should have been at a 7 or above. Keep walking on the sunny side of the street.

> **Step 2**   **Choose and Commit**
> *Choose one of the following strategies or create one of your own for the upcoming week and schedule it in your planner. Be sure to choose a reward.*

So, How Can I Be a Ten?

Increasing your optimism takes patience and perseverance. But, as any optimist knows, it's not all that difficult and anyone can do it!

Strategy #1 – Cognitive Repair
15 minutes

Raise your awareness about your thoughts and self-talk. Before you can make any change, you must first take a step back and become an observer of your inner dialogues. In your journal or in journal page at the end of this chapter, keep a diary of your thoughts and self-talk for a day or two. Go back and see what the patterns of negativity are.

Then develop a positive counter-message or thought for each negative one. For Example,

> Negative self-talk: "I'll never get that promotion. I'm just not as aggressive as I should be."

> Replaced with: "There's absolutely no reason why I won't get that promotion. I have some real strengths that the job calls for."

Strategy # 2 – Be Grateful
5 minutes

When you get up in the morning, think of 5 things that you are grateful for. Keep these in mind throughout the day. You can even jot them down on post-it notes and paste them on your bathroom mirror.

Strategy # 3 – Optimism Enhancer
5 minutes

Develop and use your own personal "Optimism Enhancer." Choose a song or fragrance that elevates your

I AM OPTIMISTIC

mood and floods your mind with positive, happy thoughts. Use your enhancer every other day first thing in the morning. Notice what's different on the days you use your enhancer. Use it throughout the day, if possible.

Do an inventory of the people closest to you in your life. Who are the most optimistic? Plan on spending more time with these people – optimism is contagious.

Step 3   **Review and Reward**
Do this on the last day of the week and be sure to reward yourself if you have succeeded.

In your journal review your progress for the week and then rate yourself:

Didn't do anything   Mastery

1............................5...............................10

Ask yourself some reflective questions such as:

- How did working on this trait make a difference in my day-to-day routine? Energy level? Relationships?
- What do I think others noticed different about me when I emulated the trait?
- How do I feel about myself when I emulate this trait?

If you rated yourself a 7 or better, you get your reward that you identified on Day One. If you didn't, don't give up. Reassess what your biggest obstacle was and make a plan to deal with it more effectively. You might want to move onto another trait and come back to this one later. Whatever you do, don't give up.

I AM OPTIMISTIC

THE HEALTHY WOMAN JOURNAL

I am Optimistic

Birds sing after a storm, why shouldn't we?
Rose Fitzgerald Kennedy

TAKE BACK YOUR LIFE NOW!

THE HEALTHY WOMAN JOURNAL

_____

_____

_____

_____

_____

_____

_____

_____

_____

_____

_____

_____

I AM SELF-ACCEPTING

*I believe that when all the dreams are dead,
you're left only with yourself.
You'd better like yourself a lot.
Rita Mae Brown*

> **Step 1** **Read, rate and reflect.**
> *Take 15 to 20 minutes on the first day of the week to complete this step.*

Ask most women, "What do you like about yourself?" and you're met with stunned silence. Ask what don't you like about yourself and the list is endless.

Most women tend to focus on their shortcomings, whether they're physical attributes or personal qualities so that they can "fix" them like a mechanic fine-tunes a car. The goal is to become more physically attractive and to better themselves - to be more loveable and respected, thus less prone to rejection or criticism. To want to be more loving or less selfish or thinner or better at tennis or cooking can either be a pattern of self-criticism and non-acceptance or one of self-improvement.

There is a difference in that self-improvement is done within a realistic framework of one's capabilities. For example, if you're not naturally athletic, beating yourself up after every mediocre tennis or golf game is a sure-fire way to diminish your self-worth and to lose your joy for the game. The road to perfection is a perilous one and one that is fraught with frustration, depression, anxiety and even self-loathing.

So, What IS Self-Acceptance?

It's very, very simple. Self-acceptance is non-judgment and it means that you're first and foremost able to recognize that you're not perfect, that you'll never be perfect and that no one else is perfect. And once you've truly realized this, you'll be able to love yourself unconditionally, warts and all. Self-acceptance does away with the rating scale you use to either measure yourself or to compare yourself to someone else.

You can dislike one of your behaviors without disliking yourself. You can even criticize or reject one of your behaviors (like smoking or not exercising) without criticizing or rejecting yourself. If you want to improve, get after your behavior and not yourself!! For example, "I need to get more exercise." versus "If I weren't so lazy, I'd exercise more." These two very different messages can leave you either with a greater sense of self-acceptance or self-criticism.

DID YOU KNOW...

According to McKay and Fanning, experts in the area of self-esteem, building self-esteem isn't just changing your critical, negative self-talk, accepting your faults, and emphasizing your good traits. The healthy, confident, woman assumes responsibility for her life by becoming a "change agent, a self-helper."

Going along with this line of thinking, Coopersmith (1967) suggested that high self-esteem/self-acceptance requires two things: setting high goals and some success in reaching your goals. In other words, you must DO SOMETHING.

The Healthy Woman Self-Rating Scale

On the Healthy Woman Rating Scale, circle where you would rate your self-acceptance level today.

1 2 3 4 5 6 7 8 9 10

I'm pitiful   **I'm my own best friend**

So, let's do a reality check on your self-rating. Answer these questions:

- Do I really know and value my strengths? (or is nothing I ever do good enough?)
- Do I accept my shortcomings with grace? (or do I say, "I'm sorry" for everything, even for breathing too loudly?)
- Do I like and accept my body? (Yes, it IS possible!)
- Do I generally forgive myself if I make a mistake or if things don't turn out perfectly?
- Can I accept criticism without becoming defensive?
- Am I able to admit when I've done something wrong and say I'm sorry? (Don't get carried away on this one. Only one "I'm sorry" a day.)

If you answered yes to the majority of the questions, you're a good friend to yourself and should have rated yourself a 7 or above.

I AM SELF-ACCEPTING

Step 2	**Choose and Commit**
	Choose one of the following strategies or create one of your own for the upcoming week and schedule it in your planner. Be sure to choose a reward.

So, How Can I Be a Ten?

Being more self-accepting requires that you make peace with yourself. When you stop struggling with who you are NOT, you can really sit back and enjoy who you ARE. Let go of the desire to be like a Martha Stewart the homemaker, or of having the face and body of a Jennifer

TAKE BACK YOUR LIFE NOW!

Aniston, or of having the job and salary of a Katie Couric. (And let's not forget the fantasy of being able to snare a mate like Brad Pitt or Mel Gibson!) It's about being at peace with your face, your body, your job, and your domestic skills - it's about liking yourself a whole lot.

Strategy #1 – Scaling Your Body
20 minutes

RE-EDUCATE YOUR EYES
First of all, you have to disarm your mirror and focus on what you DO like about your body so your reflection becomes a source of joy.

Complete the body-esteem scale. This exercise will help you break the habit of critically dissecting and judging your body. You need to re-educate your eyes so that you can see your body as a whole. The scale will help you to identify those features and body parts you DO like. Every one of us can find something we like about our bodies. It's a choice we make.

Once you complete the scale, which body parts have you rated a 7 or better? Whenever a self-criticism is leveled at any lower ranked body part, agree to focus on one of these body parts that are acceptable and affirm it.

Sprinkle your mirror with 2 or 3 Post-its with messages that affirm your body (even the one in your purse and the one on the sun visor in your car.)

Body parts to be scaled: 1= dislike; 10 = WOW!

Hair	Upper Arms	Toes
Eyes	Elbows	Back
Eyebrows	Forearms	Derriere

I AM SELF-ACCEPTING

Forehead	Wrists	Height
Nose	Hands	Weight
Fingernails	Fingers	Body
Frame	Complexion	Chin
Ears	Neck	Lips
Upper Abdomen	Lower Abdomen	Eyebrows
Teeth	Thighs	Shoulders
Calves	Breasts	Ankles

Strategy # 2 – Reprogram Your Body Talk
10 minutes

Many of our opinions about ourselves have been greatly influenced by those early messages we heard from our family while we were growing up. "Don't be so selfish!" "You're lazy just like your grandmother." We need to upgrade this outdated software.

Keep track of the more negative messages about yourself or one of your qualities that float around your brain for one day by writing each one down in your journal or in the Healthy Woman Journal at the end of this chapter. Then identify the source and do a reality check for its relevance today.

Strategy # 3 – Repattern Your Thoughts
15 minutes

"Thinking makes it so." Our repeated thoughts become ingrained into our consciousness and greatly influence our self-esteem. What kind of thoughts are you feeding your brain today?

Visualize, visualize, visualize. Practice visualizations for increasing self-acceptance. Visualize yourself appreciating your body, walking confidently and with a sense of pleasure at your uniqueness. The mind does

TAKE BACK YOUR LIFE NOW!

not recognize the difference between reality and imagination. Visualizations overwrite the negative patterns of thought. Athletes use this technique with great success.

10 minutes

Develop some affirmations by writing a thank you letter to yourself for all that you have accomplished in your life.

15 minutes

Write a letter of apology to those parts of yourself and/or your body you have been most critical and unaccepting of.

15 minutes

Ask three people you trust and respect to write a letter to you telling you what they most appreciate about you. Read their letters out loud to someone else you trust. Allow yourself to absorb the feedback.

I AM SELF-ACCEPTING

> **Step 3** **<u>Review and Reward</u>**
> *Do this on the last day of the week and be sure to reward yourself if you have succeeded.*

In your journal review your progress for the week and then rate yourself:

Didn't do anything   Mastery

1............................5................................10

Ask yourself some reflective questions such as:

- How did working on this trait make a difference in my day-to-day routine? Energy level? Relationships?
- What do I think others noticed different about me when I emulated the trait?
- How do I feel about myself when I emulate this trait?

If you rated yourself a 7 or better, you get your reward that you identified on Day One. If you didn't, don't give up. Reassess what your biggest obstacle was and make a plan to deal with it more effectively. You might want to move onto another trait and come back to this one later. Whatever you do, don't give up.

TAKE BACK YOUR LIFE NOW!

THE HEALTHY WOMAN JOURNAL

I am Self-Accepting

The hardest years in life are those between ten and seventy.
Helen Hayes

I AM SELF-NURTURING

*To keep a lamp burning,
we have to keep putting oil in it.*
Mother Teresa

*TAKE BACK YOUR LIFE **NOW!***

> **Step 1** **Read, rate and reflect.**
> *Take 15 to 20 minutes on the first day of the week to complete this step.*

What are the ways you take care of yourself? You say, "Who are you kidding? With all I have to do, I don't have time to take care of myself!"

Or do you often wonder, "How do other women get to the good stuff?" – the warm bubble bath, the quiet cozy corner with a book. Isn't that being selfish? NO! It's definitely not!

You actually have a *responsibility* to first and foremost take care of yourself - to develop the trait of self-nurturance. This is radical thinking for most women. "How can I put my needs before my kids' needs or my partner's or my boss' or my parents'?" "I would feel so guilty since that would make me a bad mom, wife, worker, daughter." "After all, I've 'got to' take care of everyone else before I 'get to' take care of me."

A well respected executive coach once told us to fill our lives with "get to's" and eliminate all of the "got to's." The "get to's" are enjoyable and rewarding things you do for yourself. Madonna is a "get to" girl. She gets to do what she loves, as much or as little as she wants and wherever in the world she wants to do it. Marie, Raymond's mother, on the other hand is a "got to" girl not only for herself but for her daughter-in-law as well! She's "got to" cook dinner, clean house, and iron underwear to feel good about herself.

Which are you? Look back on what you did for the past week. Take a moment to evaluate how you might change that ratio.

Keep in mind, however, the amount of time available for your "get to's" will be different, depending on the stage of life you're in. It's quality, not quantity. If you're parenting small children, getting up a half an hour early to have some quiet time is a very realistic "get to." If you're an empty–nester, you might take an hour or two.

Remember the old adage, "When mommy's happy, everybody's happy." If you're meeting your needs and nurturing yourself, your family will benefit more than you can ever imagine.

One woman we worked with was very good at self-nurturing. She was a high-powered management consultant who traveled week after week to new project sites where she worked long hours in stressful environments.

Navigating overcrowded airports, living in cookie-cutter hotels with bad carpeting, and attending endless meetings away from her family was a way of life. In spite of it all, she found one small thing that made a big difference in her life.

Once a week, instead of going to dinner and drinks with the project team, she made an appointment to have her nails done. Yes, have her nails done. There she met other women with whom she could talk about her kids, commiserate about in-laws and compare stories about hubbies. She loved sharing laughs and life's ups and downs. This small get-a-way infused her life with energy that spilled over to her job and her family life and had a positive effect.

The Healthy Woman Self-Rating Scale

On the Healthy Woman Rating Scale below, circle where you would rate your self-nurturing level today.

I don't matter　　　　　　　**I make time for me**

So, let's do a reality check on your self-rating. Here are some questions to help you reflect on your ability to self-nurture:

- Do I make excuses when it comes to nurturing myself? ("It's too late." "I'm too tired." "Why bother?")
- Do I feel selfish and guilty when I take time to nurture myself? (Remember, "When mommy's happy, everyone's happy!")
- Do I see this self-nurturing trait as a sign of self-indulgence? (Me, me, me and nobody else but me.)
- Is it difficult to define what would actually be nurturing to me? (Do I remember what that feels like?)

If you've answered yes to the questions, you should have rated yourself a 4 or below.

A Self-Nurturing Evaluation

The statements below describe the ways we can nurture ourselves.
As you read each one, rate yourself from 1 (I don't do this at all = ☹) to 5 (I do this frequently and on a regular basis = ☺)

I AM SELF-NURTURING

Nurturing the body

1. Take time to de-stress the body by exercise, yoga, eating healthy, not smoking, limiting alcohol, meditation breaks, and stress management.

     1...2...3...4...5
     ☹   ☺

2. Make a commitment to do your annual 100,000 mile check-up like having your mammogram, a pap smear, 6 month dental check-ups, cholesterol checks, blood pressure checks, colonoscopy, etc. Rate yourself:

     1...2...3...4...5
     ☹   ☺

3. Pamper your body with manicures, facials, massages and pedicures. Rate yourself:

     1...2...3...4...5
     ☹   ☺

4. Tune into your senses. What scents do you find pleasurable? Freshly cut grass? What textures do you like to touch and feel? Velvet? A dog's nose? What tastes are pleasurable to you? Sweet or salty? What sights and sounds create a sense of peace and well-being? The ocean, a sunset, a stream. Rate yourself:

     1...2...3...4...5

TAKE BACK YOUR LIFE NOW!

☹   ☺

5. Have a feelings journal. Use it to write down your feelings or to draw them. Feelings are an energy and need an outlet. Be kind to them and let them go and you will feel a lightness and overall sense of well being

1...2...3...4...5
☹   ☺

Nurturing the self/spirit

6. Be kind and affectionate to yourself. Make time to, as Mother Teresa says, put oil in your lamp so you burn brightly. Connect with your sense of purpose and your spiritual path, whatever that may be.

1...2...3...4...5
☹   ☺

7. Spend time with nature. Take walks in a park; observe birds, butterflies, and squirrels. Feel the joy in being alive

1...2...3...4...5
☹   ☺

Total your scores. Kudos to you if you scored 25 to 35! Keep up the good work. 15-20 isn't too bad! Anything below, "Nurture thyself."!!!!

I AM SELF-NURTURING

Step 2	**Choose and Commit**
	Choose one of the following strategies or create one of your own for the upcoming week and schedule it in your planner. Be sure to choose a reward.

So, How Can I Be a Ten?

Being a ten on the self-nurturance scale requires that you value yourself enough to make the time to be self-nurturing.

Strategy # 1 Step Up to the Plate

Because this is a difficult trait for most women, let's use the self-rating scale above to help you develop some goals. Where did you rate yourself in terms of your degree of self-nurturance?
15 minutes

If you rated yourself a 4 or below, start by thinking what types of activities are nurturing to you. Make a list. This is the first step in developing this trait.

If you rated yourself a 5, 6, or 7 you will have to learn to live with the initial guilt feelings you might experience when you self-nurture. Guilt never killed anybody. So when you're self-nurturing, use your guilt as a good sign that you're doing what you're supposed to be doing!

If you rated yourself an 8, 9 or 10, help the other women in your life to be more self-nurturing. Sometimes all a woman needs is permission from someone she loves, respects and trusts.

Strategy #2 – Stream of Consciousness
15 minutes

Brainstorm a list of activities that are energizing and nurturing for you. Don't limit yourself! Be creative and write anything down that comes to mind. In your journal or in the journal page at the end of this chapter, write them down. Go over and mark the ones that are achievable with an X. Select two of these and in your daily planner, schedule these alternately for the next three weeks. Remember, when you write it down, you are making a commitment to yourself. Share this with a friend and have her follow-up on your progress.

Strategy #3 – Oil Change and Lube Job for the Body
10 minutes

In your daily planner, schedule your yearly check-ups near or around your birthday. Call your respective physicians and make the appointments. If you don't have a Primary Care Physician and a gynecologist, find one and set up a time to meet and "interview" this person to make sure he or she is a good fit with your personality and style of communication.

> # Step 3 Review and Reward
> *Do this on the last day of the week and be sure to reward yourself if you have succeeded.*

In your journal review your progress for the week and then rate yourself:

Didn't do anything   Mastery

1..............................5................................10

Ask yourself some reflective questions such as:

- How did working on this trait make a difference in my day-to-day routine? Energy level? Relationships?
- What do I think others noticed different about me when I emulated the trait?
- How do I feel about myself when I emulate this trait?

If you rated yourself a 7 or better, you get your reward that you identified on Day One. If you didn't, don't give up.

Reassess what your biggest obstacle was and make a plan to deal with it more effectively. You might want to move onto another trait and come back to this one later. Whatever you do, don't give up.

I AM SELF-NURTURING

THE HEALTHY WOMAN JOURNAL

I am Self-Nurturing

I hate housework! You make the beds,
you do the dishes and six months later
you have to start all over again.
Joan Rivers

TAKE BACK YOUR LIFE NOW!

THE HEALTHY WOMAN JOURNAL

I AM SPIRITUAL

Spirituality is a kind of virgin wisdom, a knowing that comes prior to experience.
Marilyn Ferguson

> **Step 1** **Read, rate and reflect.**
> *Take 15 to 20 minutes on the first day of the week to complete this step.*

What does being spiritual mean to you? This is a very difficult question that can have many different answers. We think most people agree that one's spirituality is unique to the individual and is a deeply personal quest.

For our purposes, let's suffice it to say that we view a woman as spiritual when she is able to simply live her life with joyfulness. Not a joy based on accomplishments or an acquisition of material things and not a joy that insulates her from the normal sorrows and disappointments of life but rather a very deep, subtle joy that is not shaken by life's challenges - a joy in her spirit and its aliveness.

In so doing, she is one who has a belief system or a faith that allows her to let go of what is not under her control, is unconditional in her love for herself and increases her sense of belonging to all of life. The spiritual woman is clear about what she needs to do to keep her spirituality alive and kicking and is committed to do whatever it takes to make this journey. This doesn't mean that she might not waver or retreat from her path periodically throughout her life. But what it does mean is that she will sooner or later come back home to it.

The Healthy Woman Self-Rating Scale

On the Healthy Woman Rating Scale below, circle where you would rate your spiritual level today.

I AM SPIRITUAL

I have no spirituality **I'm a spiritual person**

So, let's do a reality check on your self-rating. Here are some questions to help you explore this side of yourself.

- Do I often feel hopeless and terribly alone?
- Do I feel as though my life is joyless?
- Do I hold onto old resentments toward the religion I grew up with?
- Do I often wonder with some despair what the point of it all is?

If you've answered yes to these questions, you need to strengthen your spiritual side and begin to define a spiritual path for yourself. You probably rated yourself a 4 or below on the self-rating scale. Once you've discovered which path brings you a sense of peace and joy in being alive, you will need to nourish that spiritual side with some type of spiritual practice such as prayer, meditation, yoga, a walk in the woods, to mention a few.

TAKE BACK YOUR LIFE NOW!

Step 2	**Choose and Commit**
	Choose one of the following strategies or create one of your own for the upcoming week and schedule it in your planner. Be sure to choose a reward.

So, How Can I Be a Ten?

Growing in your spirituality requires that you make the time to explore your values and principles and then find a spiritual practice that will support these values and then commit yourself to it. A spiritual side will definitely promote optimism, joy, a sense of peace and inner contentment.

Strategy #1 – Find Your Joyfulness
15 minutes

In your journal or in the journal page at the end of this chapter, do the following exercise:

- On a scale of 1 to 10, with one being Not at All Joyful and 10 being Extremely Joyful, what's the highest you've ever been on that scale?
- When was that? What were you doing? Who were you with?
- By reflecting on these questions, you can try to determine when you experienced your spiritual side. This can be a beginning in being able to nurture this part of yourself by repeating these experiences.

You can do the same exercise using Peace as the feeling being measured.

Strategy #2 – Self-Educate
45 minutes

If you are uncertain as to how to explore this part of yourself talk to a minister, therapist, or good friend who exhibits the "joy" and "peace" you are seeking. Discuss your feelings, ideas, etc., and begin journaling your new awarenesses.

Read spiritual books or listen to audiotapes and learn about different spiritual practices. As you read, journal your reactions or talk with someone you trust.

Visit various churches and see which service and community you feel most comfortable with.

TAKE BACK YOUR LIFE NOW!

Strategy #3 – Decide What's Right For You
30 minutes

If the idea of "church" or a spiritual practice is unappealing to you, consider spending quiet time in nature. Hiking, walking or just meditating in the open can bring a sense of peace and joy. The goal is to experience the complete joy of being alive. And remember, a spiritual path is a process…not an event. So be patient and open to the possibilities.

> **Step 3**   **Review and Reward**
> *Do this on the last day of the week and be sure to reward yourself if you have succeeded.*

In your journal review your progress for the week and then rate yourself:

Didn't do anything   Mastery

1……………………………5……………………………10

Ask yourself some reflective questions such as:

- How did working on this trait make a difference in my day-to-day routine? Energy level? Relationships?
- What do I think others noticed different about me when I emulated the trait?
- How do I feel about myself when I emulate this trait?

If you rated yourself a 7 or better, you get your reward that you identified on Day One. If you didn't, don't give up. Reassess what your biggest obstacle was and make a plan to deal with it more effectively. You might want to move onto another trait and come back to this one later. Whatever you do, don't give up.

TAKE BACK YOUR LIFE NOW!

THE HEALTHY WOMAN JOURNAL

I am Spiritual

It must be Sunday. Everybody is telling the truth.
Phoebe Snow

Final Thoughts

Well, it's been quite a journey! You are to be congratulated for completing the program. You are on your way to taking your life back and being the healthiest woman you know! In many of the keynote addresses I give (BMc), I encourage the women who attend to say this mantra out loud every single day—"I AM MY MOST IMPORTANT PERSON." I'm asking you to do the same. I'm confident that this program has not only given you the confidence to say it, but also to truly believe it.

*TAKE BACK YOUR LIFE **NOW!***

We hope that the past ten weeks have opened your eyes to how vital and vibrant you can be. But like anything worth having, you must keep at it.

Use this book over and over again. You may just want to work on one trait for a few weeks or a month rather than go through the whole program again. You may want to pick up the book if you've had some significant life changes such as a new baby, a marriage or an empty nest. Significant changes frequently precipitate a regression to old behaviors or attitudes. Remember, it's easy to forget just how important you should be to yourself – but even more so in times of change. The Today's Healthy Woman Poster and Tip Sheet can keep you on track and strengthen your commitment, so be sure to keep them visible. We know that by mastering these ten traits, you will enhance your life significantly and this will positively affect all of your relationships.

If you completed this program successfully, please notify us at our website **www.healthyinspiration.com** and we'll send you a reward of our own! All we ask is that you tell us in 25 words or less how the program has helped you and made a difference in your life.

You can also check our website periodically for more tips and strategies, resource information and just to say Hi and let us know how you're doing. You can share any strategies or tips that would help other women become living examples of Today's Healthy Woman!

Here's wishing you the best of health and happiness!

Dr. Barbara McFarland   Mr. Steve Wuest
Psychologist   Coach and Mentor

Educational Tools

Healthy Inspiration has developed some complementary tools that you can use in conjunction with this book. You can find more information on these by visiting our website at **www.healthyinspiration.com.**

The Today's Healthy Woman Poster

12x36 Full Color Poster comes with Gray Border or Purple Border

This poster is illustrated by Pulitzer Prize winning editorial cartoonist Ann Telnaes and the poster depicts the ten traits. Display the poster where you can see it (i.e., refrigerator, laundry room, office, etc.) on a daily basis to remind you to focus on the traits and to take care of yourself.

Spanish poster soon to be released (check website for date)

The Today's Healthy Woman Tip Sheet

This 8 ½ by 11 laminated reminder provides practical 60 second strategies for each of the ten traits and complements the poster. It is great for your planner or cubicle wall. No excuse not remember to take care of yourself

FOR TEACHERS AND COUNSELORS

The Today's Healthy Woman Lesson Plans and Discussion Guide

This 20-page, 2-color booklet is great for use with girls in grades 9-12. Eleven lesson plans and three overheads make learning about health challenging and fun. We've developed an adjunct lesson plan for boys which allows the teacher/counselor to customize the ten traits just for them.

The Healthy Teen Tip Sheet

This 8 ½ by 11 reminder provides 20 fun and practical strategies related to the ten traits and is an effective tool encouraging self-responsibility for teen girls. Great for the bulletin board, notebook, or bedroom wall.

Teacher's Kit (combines three great products)

12 x 36 Today's Healthy Woman Full Color Poster
11 Lesson Plans and Discussion Guide
Package of 30 Healthy Teen Tip Sheets

FOR MOMS AND DAUGHTERS

Discussion Guide for Moms and Daughters

A creative program designed to encourage "chats" between moms and daughters. It includes guidelines for *when* to talk to your daughter and *how* to talk to her. It includes powerful techniques, discussion questions and goal setting strategies intended to enhance your relationship with your daughter and to help her be her healthiest for the rest of her life.

Mother/Daughter Kit (combines three great products)

12 x 36 Today's Healthy Woman Full Color Poster
Discussion Guide for Moms and Daughters
Healthy Teen 2 color Tip Sheet

Healthy Woman Check-up Stickers

A unique "reminder" to help make sure you get your annual check-ups for mammograms, pap smears, dental check-ups, vision, etc. Look at our website for release date.

Visit www.healthyinspiration.com or call 513-943-1946 for more information.

About the Authors

Dr. McFarland, EdD, is a psychologist, author, trainer, media guest, and motivational speaker who has been enhancing the lives of women for nearly 25 years. Barbara has authored 7 other books and written many articles on various women's issues, the most recent on body image was published in *Oprah Magazine.* In addition, she counsels women and teen-age girls in her private practice and has done so for nearly 25 years. She was a pioneer in the area of women and addiction, was invited to present her clinical work at Harvard University Medical School, conducted corporate training classes as part of the Xavier Consulting Group, and presented keynote speeches at many women's health conferences. She has appeared on Oprah, The Today Show, National Public Radio as well as many others. Barbara, mother to a great son and daughter-in-law, lives on a farm in Kentucky with her husband, Harold, and their awesome dog, Fred.

Steve Wuest is a successful management consultant and executive coach with over 25 years of experience in his field. Mr. Wuest spent almost 20 years in the performance improvement practice of Deloitte & Touche and, as a partner he provided leadership to the practice in the areas of recruiting, personnel development, client service, business planning, and business development. He headed up the Midwest health care consulting practice at one time and served such prestigious health care providers as the Cleveland Clinic, the Detroit Medical Center, Methodist Hospital of Indianapolis, Strong Memorial Hospital in Rochester, Children's Hospital and many others. He has counseled, guided, and inspired hundreds of women professionals and entrepreneurs during that time. He is the proud father of a daughter and a son.

The Artist

Ms. Ann Telnaes serves as a design consultant to Healthy Inspiration. In that capacity she drew all of the cartoons and illustrations in the Today's Healthy Woman poster and **Take Back Your Life NOW!** In 2001, she became the second woman to win a Pulitzer Prize for editorial cartooning. Ann's editorial cartoons have appeared in such prestigious publications as The Chicago Tribune, The Washington Post, The Los Angeles Times, St. Louis Post-Dispatch Newsday, The New York Times, The Baltimore Sun, Austin American Statesman and USA Today.

Printed in the United States
1271000005BA/115-285